Downers Grove Public Library

1050 Curtiss St.

Downers Grove, IL 60515

(630) 960-1200

www.downersgrovelibrary.org

11/14-22

GAYLORD

Earth
The Blue Planet

By Daisy Allyn

Gareth Stevens
Publishing

Please visit our Web site, www.garethstevens.com. For a free color catalog of all our high-quality books, call toll free 1-800-542-2595 or fax 1-877-542-2596.

Library of Congress Cataloging-in-Publication Data

Allyn, Daisy.
 Earth : the blue planet / Daisy Allyn.
    p. cm. — (Our solar system)
 Includes bibliographical references and index.
 ISBN 978-1-4339-3819-1 (pbk. : alk. paper)
 ISBN 978-1-4339-3820-7 (6-pack)
 ISBN 978-1-4339-3818-4 (library binding : alk. paper)
 1. Earth—Juvenile literature. I. Title.
 QB631.4.A35 2010
 525—dc22

                              2010000487

First Edition

Published in 2011 by
Gareth Stevens Publishing
111 East 14th Street, Suite 349
New York, NY 10003

Copyright © 2011 Gareth Stevens Publishing

Designer: Christopher Logan
Editor: Greg Roza

Photo credits: Cover, back cover, p. 1 Photodisc; p. 5 © Calvin J. Hamilton; p. 7 NASA; pp. 9, 11, 13, 15 (all), 17 (all), 21 Shutterstock.com; p. 19 NASA/MODIS/USGS.

Printed in the United States of America

CPSIA compliance information: Batch #CS10GS: For further information contact Gareth Stevens, New York, New York at 1-800-542-2595.

Contents

Boldface words appear in the glossary.

Home Sweet Home!

Earth is the third planet from the sun. It is where we live. Earth is the only planet in the **solar system** with plants and animals.

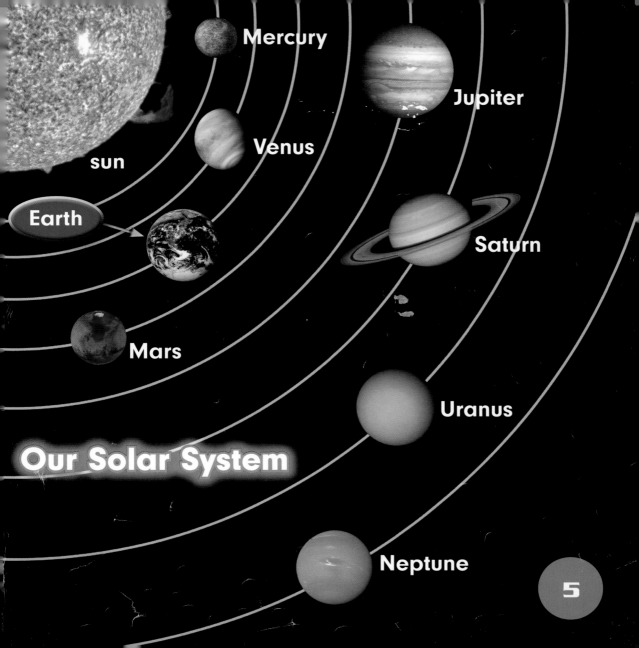

Mercury

sun

Venus

Jupiter

Earth

Saturn

Mars

Uranus

Our Solar System

Neptune

5

To someone in space, Earth looks blue. This is because water covers most of Earth. Someone in space may also see green and brown land. They may see white clouds, too.

7

Move It!

Earth **orbits** the sun. It takes about 365 days, or 1 year, to orbit the sun. Earth also spins around. Earth takes about 24 hours, or 1 day, to spin around once.

sun

Earth

The Moon

Earth has one moon. The moon orbits Earth once every 28 days. The moon looks different to people on Earth at different times during its orbit.

11

In the Air

Earth's air makes it a special planet. Plants, animals, and people need to breathe Earth's air to live. Air also helps make weather.

13

On the Ground

We live on Earth's **crust**. The crust has mountains, deserts, forests, and oceans. What does Earth's crust look like where you live?

mountains

forest

desert

ocean

15

People use Earth's crust to live. We build towns and cities on Earth's crust. We grow crops in the crust. We take things like **metal** and oil out of Earth's crust.

town

crops

oil

metal

17

Inside Earth

Beneath Earth's crust is the mantle. The mantle is made of soft, hot rock. Earth's center is called the core. Earth's core is made of metal.

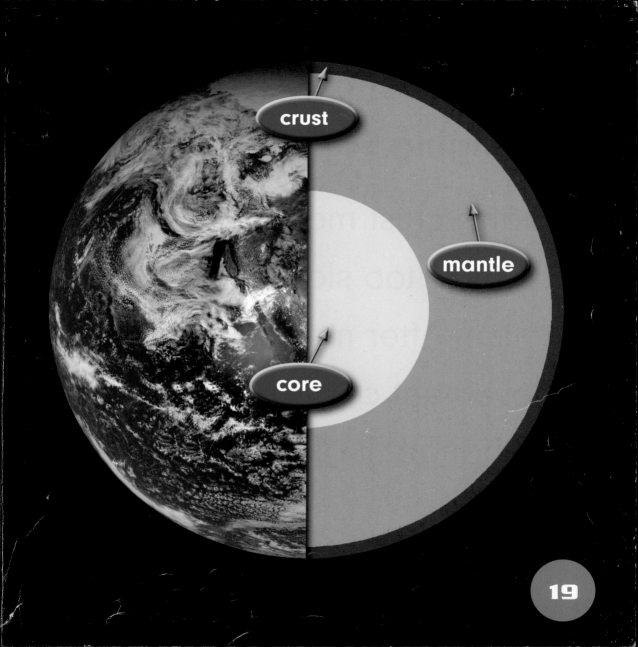

crust

mantle

core

Changing Earth

Earth's crust moves very slowly. It moves too slowly for us to notice. After many years, this movement causes Earth's land to change. It also causes **earthquakes** and **volcanoes**!

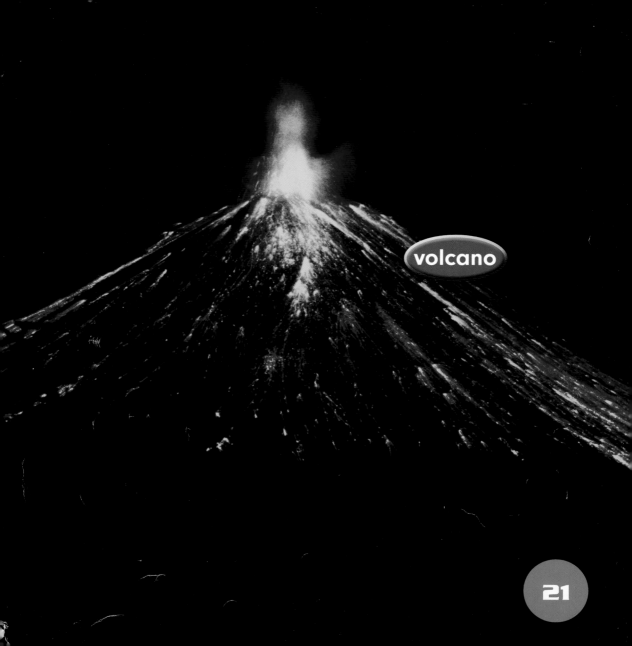

volcano

21

Glossary

crust: the outer shell of a planet

earthquake: a rumbling of the ground caused by the movement of Earth's crust

metal: a shiny rock, like iron or gold, found in Earth's crust

orbit: to travel in a circle or oval around something

solar system: the sun and all the space objects that orbit it, including the planets and their moons

volcano: an opening in a planet's surface through which hot, liquid rock sometimes flows

For More Information

Books

Asch, Frank. *The Earth and I*. Orlando, FL: Voyager Books, 2008.

Green, Jen. *Children's Planet Earth Encyclopedia*. New York, NY: Parragon, 2008.

Pratt, Leonie. *Planet Earth*. Eveleth, MN: Usborne Books, 2007.

Web Sites

For Kids Only: Earth Science

kids.earth.nasa.gov

NASA's Earth science site for kids contains facts about the people, land, air, water, and dangers of planet Earth.

How Volcanoes Work

science.howstuffworks.com/volcano.htm

Read all about volcanoes and how they are formed by Earth's forces.

Index

About the Author

Daisy Allyn teaches chemistry and physics at a small high school in western New York. A science teacher by day, Allyn spends many nights with her telescope, exploring the solar system. Her Great Dane, Titan, often joins Allyn on her nightly star-gazing missions.